MW01103879

My Healthy Food Pyramid

By
Diane H. Pappas & Richard D. Covey

Illustrated by
Ric Estrada

SCHOLASTIC INC.
New York Toronto London Auckland Sydney
Mexico City New Delhi Hong Kong Buenos Aires

Dear Parents:

This book is our opportunity to provide you with an important educational tool—"The Healthy Food Pyramid." We hope you will use this book to introduce your children to a lifelong practice of healthy eating. The Healthy Food Pyramid offers healthy eating guidelines based on decades of quality scientific study.

Explain to your children that the pyramid shape suggests that the healthiest and most nutritious foods that should be eaten are shown at the big base of the pyramid; the tiny tip indicates the foods that should be eaten only occasionally.

We thank Dr. Walter C. Willett, M. D., Chairman of the Department of Nutrition, Harvard Medical School, and creator of The Healthy Eating Pyramid, for his support and permission to use his pyramid.

No part of this publication may be reproduced, stored in a retrieval system, or transmitted in any form or by any means, electronic, mechanical, photocopying, recording, or otherwise, without written permission of the publisher. For information regarding permission, write to Scholastic Inc., Attention: Permissions Department, 557 Broadway, New York, NY 10012.

ISBN-13: 978-0-545-01429-8
ISBN-10: 0-545-01429-8

Text and Illustration copyright © 2007 by A G Education, Inc.

The Harvard Healthy Eating Pyramid appears courtesy of EAT, DRINK, AND BE HEALTHY by Walter C. Willet, M.D. Copyright © 2001, 2005 by President and Fellows of Harvard College. Reprinted with permission of Simon & Schuster Adult Publishing Group.

All rights reserved. Published by Scholastic Inc.
Kid Guardians®, Kid Guardians® Just Be Healthy Series™, and associated logos are trademarks and/or registered trademarks of D. H. Pappas and/or A G Education, Inc. SCHOLASTIC and associated logos are trademarks and/or registered trademarks of Scholastic Inc.

12 11 10 9 8 7 6 5 4 3 2 1   7 8 9 10 11 12/0
Printed in the U.S.A.
First printing, October 2007

Note to parents and teachers: Please read this page to your children and students to introduce them to the Kid Guardians.

MEET THE KID GUARDIANS

From their home base in the mystical Himalayan mountain kingdom of Shambala, Zak the Yak and the Kid Guardians are always on alert, ready to protect the children of the world from danger.

 ZAK THE YAK is a gentle giant with a heart of gold. He's the leader of the Kid Guardians.

 Loyal and lovable, **SCRUBBER** is Zak's best friend and sidekick.

 BUZZER is both street-smart and book-smart, with a real soft spot for kids.

 Always curious about the world, **SMOOCH** loves to meet new people and see new places.

 CARROT, with her wild red hair, is funny, lovable, and the first to jump in when help is needed.

 Whenever a child is in danger, the **TROUBLE BUBBLE**™ sounds an alarm and then instantly transports the Kid Guardians to that location.

Today, Ms. Garcia begins her class nutrition lesson. . . .
"This summer vacation I visited the Egyptian pyramids,"
said Ms. Garcia.
"Why are we talking about pyramids?" asked Tommy.

"Zak, let's help Ms. Garcia's class," begged Carrot. "Please, Zak?"
"OK, Carrot, let's go!"

"Hi, kids, I'm Zak and this is Carrot. We came to help with the lesson," Zak said.

"What a surprise," said Ms. Garcia with a smile. "We always welcome your help, Zak."

Zak pulled out his Z-pad.

"Tommy, we're going to show you what pyramids have to do with nutrition," said Zak. "Just take a look at the back of the room."

"The bottom of The Healthy Food Pyramid shows things you need every day. The top shows what you should eat in small amounts," explained Zak.

White Rice, Potato, Sweets

Red Meat, Butter

Dairy (Calcium Supplement)

Fish, Poultry, Eggs

Nuts, Legumes

Vegetables

Fruits

Whole Grains

Plant Oils (Olive, Canola, Soy)

Daily Exercise and Weight Control

"Wow!" said Josh.

"Look," said Ms. Garcia, "the base of the pyramid is daily exercise. That's because exercise is very important."

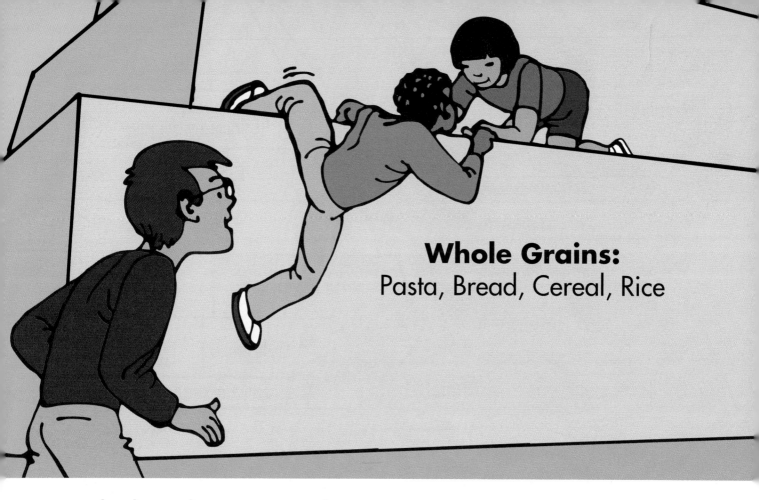

Whole Grains:
Pasta, Bread, Cereal, Rice

"Let's climb to the top," said Mia.
"Come on!" said Carrot. "Whole wheat bread, oatmeal, and brown rice are just a few of the whole-grain carbohydrates. They'll give you the energy to get up the pyramid."

Fruits, Vegetables

"Vegetables and fresh fruit are really important and taste great. They make their own special chemicals, vitamins, and minerals that help protect you from getting sick. So eat some every day," Zak said.

"Awesome," exclaimed Tommy. "I love carrots."

Nuts, Legumes

"Oh, boy! Peanuts are my favorite," Josh said.
"These beans taste great in burritos," said Mia.
"And they're full of protein, vitamins, and minerals,"
said Ms. Garcia.
"Zak, what are proteins?" asked Josh.

Fish, Poultry, Eggs

"Josh, proteins are the building blocks that make your bones and muscles grow. Protein also repairs cuts, scrapes, and broken bones," replied Zak. "All the foods on this level give you protein."

Dairy:
Milk, Cheese

"Cold milk really tastes good," Mia said.
"Milk and cheese contain calcium. That makes bones grow strong," said Zak. "You should drink three glasses of low fat or skim milk a day while you are growing. Now you've all earned a treat! Let's climb to the top."

Sweets, Potatoes

"The tip of the pyramid has the food types that we should eat only once in a while, in small amounts," advised Carrot. "French fries, chips, and ice cream should only be eaten as snacks. But once in a while we all need a treat, so enjoy the ice cream."

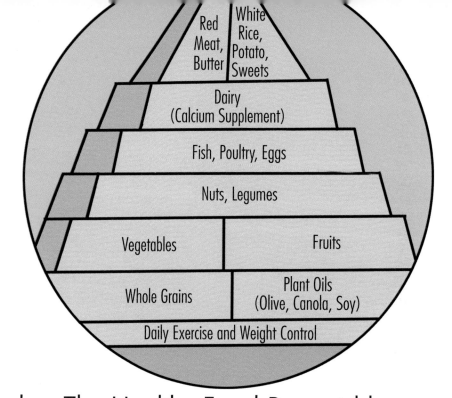

Red Meat, Butter

White Rice, Potato, Sweets

Dairy
(Calcium Supplement)

Fish, Poultry, Eggs

Nuts, Legumes

Vegetables

Fruits

Whole Grains

Plant Oils
(Olive, Canola, Soy)

Daily Exercise and Weight Control

Let's remember The Healthy Food Pyramid lessons. . . .

1. Eat more food at the bottom of the pyramid and less from the top
2. Brown rice, oatmeal, and whole wheat bread are complex carbohydrates that give you energy.
3. Eat vegetables and fruit daily.
4. Your body gets protein from nuts, beans, chicken, eggs, and fish.
5. Calcium makes your bones thick and strong.